Hush No More
A Poetry Book

Healing Through Words

Authored & Compiled by
DR. VANESSA DUNN GUYTON

Edited by
Robin D. Whitehead Rudolph

No part of this publication may be reproduced or transmitted in any form or by any means, electronic or mechanical, including photocopy, recording, or any information from the publisher, except for brief quotations used in critical articles and reviews.

Printed in the United States of America Copyright © Vanessa Dunn Guyton, 2022 All Rights Reserved

Published by Consulting Experts & Associates, 261 Business Park Blvd., Columbia, SC 29229

The information in this book is designed to both provide helpful information on the subjects discussed and motivate readers to action. This book is not meant to be used as a tool to diagnose or treat any psychological condition. It is sold with the understanding that the authors and publisher are not engaged to render any type of psychological, legal, or any other kind of professional advice. The content is the sole expression and opinion of its authors. Neither the publisher nor the authors shall be liable for any physical, psychological, emotional, financial, or commercial damages incurred as a result of this text. You are responsible for your own choices, actions, and results. Only you can make the life you want.

YOU ARE NOT ALONE...Help is available.

ACKNOWLEDGEMENTS

A big thank-you goes to our amazing Creator, our Ancestors, and my parents, Freddie, and Geneva Dunn. I promise to continue making you proud by being a positive force for good in this world.

My heart will always be held by my children, Keith, Teaira, Tony, Miata, and De'Quan, and my grandchildren, Braylin, Jeremiah, and Phoenix. As I continue to heal, I pray that we grow closer and that you continue advocating for others.

I owe many of my successes in large part to my amazing Life and Success Strategist Coach, Your guidance, patience, gifts, and wisdom have contributed significantly the 'HUSH No More' book, documentary, and movement. For that, I will always be grateful and thankful to have you in my life.

A special thank-you goes to all my friends who helped me through my trauma by listening and actively supporting me: Angela, Shai, CJ, Valerie, Tasha, Erica, and Tony.

I am grateful for the women of the Spiritual Progress Alcoholic Anonymous Group in Columbia, SC. Thank you for sharing your journey with me. We will change the world, by remaining sober.

To the man who raped me, thank you for helping me find my purpose and change the world.

DEDICATION

This project is dedicated to the authors of this book for your courage and strength to overcome your trauma, and for your willingness to help others by deciding that you will HUSH No More because YOU HAVE A RIGHT TO TELL IT. Your poetry is life changing.

Additionally, to all past and future victims of the HUSH topics who find their voice and courage to become survivors; may this book serve as a reminder that you are not alone and you have a right to tell it and heal!

Lastly, to my grandmother, Bessie Lee Overstreet Anderson and my favorite cousin, Barbara Jean Pritchett (Bop). Knowing that you both survived your HUSH Topics with courage, during a time that no one was allowed to share their trauma. I thank you for sharing with me and deciding to HUSH No More. I will continue fighting for women and men who were forbidden to tell.

CONTENTS

Introduction/Purpose 1
Our Right to Tell It 3
Domestic Violence 5
   A Victim of False Love 5
   BUT I LOVE YOU! 9
   Aftermath 11
   The Color of Love 14
   Learned Behavior 16

Sexual Assault 19
   There's Nothing Inspirational About Rape 19
   Hear Me 22
   Betrayed 25
   My Inception 27
   Sleepless: The Invisible Scar No One Can See 29
   Can You Hear Me Now?? 35
   Bye Bye Nikki 37

Child Sexual Abuse 42
   I Never Told 42
   I WAS 44
   MY BODY IS MY BODY 45
   Me Too 47
   Molested 50

    Between Sisters 52
    Dancing In The Rain 53
    Journey to an Internal Place 56
    Innocent Souls 60
    Choices 63

Sexual Harassment 68
    Unemployed 68
    Penetration 69

Human Trafficking 71
    Before It Had a Name 71
    The Game 76

Dr. Guyton's Right to Tell It 82
    R. Kelly vs. India Arie 82
    After Trauma vs. After Healing 85
    Antidepressant Medication 87
    Butterfly Freedom 88
    Sexual Slaves-A Perspective From My Ancestors 89
    Heartbreak & Rebirth 92
    Falling In Love Again 94

Support/ Words of Encouragement 96
    My Daily Affirmation 97
    Better Days 99
    I AM 100

> Friends 102
>
> You Are 103
>
> Lord 104

Friends & Family Support 110
Definitions 113
Support Hotline Numbers 121
About the Author 123
Contributing Authors: 125

Introduction/Purpose

The HUSH No More Movement was created to elevate awareness of the negative impacts that sexual assault, sexual harassment, domestic violence, sex trafficking, and other violent crimes have had on the lives of victims. This is a rapidly growing movement to bring awareness that will lead to the prevention and ultimate end of all those aforementioned, horrible acts. Our goal here is to provide an active outlet for survivors to share their stories of pain, betrayal, abuse, and most important, growth. By sharing the stories of some fearless survivors who dared to stand tall and share their truth, we hope to inspire others to muster the strength to overcome all the social stigmas and shame, survive, and thrive with the incredible resilience of love and forgiveness.

Each year, millions of individuals fall victim to heinous sexual crimes and domestic violence, which often goes unreported. These victims, young and old, male, and female, of every race and background, frequently go years without telling anyone of the trauma they've experienced at the hands of their perpetrators.

Many have taken their pain to their graves while many others live among us, work with us, pray with us, and walk by us every day without as much as a whisper about the hell they are experiencing in their lives.

Some fear their perpetrators and abusers, others hold a fear of shame, and many simply fear not being believed.

While this gripping fear has silenced many of their voices, now we are encouraging victims to become survivors by Helping Unleash the Shame to Heal and providing advocacy services and training that hopefully lead to the prevention of all the HUSH Topics.

Our Right to Tell It

Society, gossip, and family pressures have created a hostile environment where victims feel as if they must hide their trauma.

This leads to feelings of shame, low self-esteem and self-worth, drug abuse, alcoholism, additional trauma, etc. Contrary to the detrimental beliefs of others, victims have a right to share exactly what happened to them and be heard. They have a right to speak or write about their trauma and their abuser. When individuals come forward and share their story, they start to heal and unleash the shame they have been experiencing. Some people may not believe their story or support them after they come forward. Regardless, it's their choice to decide when, how, and if they will ever share their story. The courageous poets in this book have decided that this is the right time for them to share their survival journey with the world to heal and to promote awareness and prevention of the HUSH Topics.

The poems you are about to read are all written and formatted by the poets, as their way of coming forward to HUSH No

More. They are raw and heartfelt and may trigger an emotional response. If this occurs, take time to journal your thoughts and contact a professional to discuss your emotions.

Domestic Violence
A Victim of False Love

Lies after Lies – she told me

I was enslaved by a demonic spirit that
worked through the love of a person who
portrayed a demisable image

I was held captive in two lost souls- mine and hers
I fought a good fight, but truthfully, I lost
against myself for trying so hard to please
her then to be a better me

She victimized me with a distasteful and
tainted love that I hate to even account for

I messed up for allowing her back into my
life thinking she had changed her defiled
and unworthy ways from before

Here we go once again!

She falsified my hopes and dreams that I
envisioned of us

My spiritual love was ridiculed and
humiliated by selfish and in secured
human specimens
They hurt me fiercely for their own
agenda and inferiorities

And manipulated my mind and strong
heart which now feels weak, but I won't
let me fall apart

I'm so sad about the situation
I'm so mad at Myself.
I know my worth is valuable and I felt as
though I let it down

I became my own prisoner and ended up
going into a brief confinement, because of
a situation that my false love provoked

I feel so ashamed and demeaned in front
of my father in heaven

Now, I have to bear witness of
consequences for something vicious that
could have been prevented

I'm waiting on the Lord to set me totally
 free from self-pity and negativity

My good character was not perfect, but I
didn't deserve to be betrayed and
disrespected by the one I loved so hard,
supported, and took care of

The relationship was laced with
impurities, insanity acts and control issues
of disobedience that my God was not
pleased with
I tried to do the right thing and guess
what; it caused me heartache, emotional
pain, failures, and major goals setbacks

I pray to God asking him for his
forgiveness as I repented for the sins that I
had committed against thee

And I personally thank him for another
chance and delivering my flesh and soul
from the Victim of False Love

Tammy Nicole Myers

Tammy Nicole Myers (Free Spirit) is a Native of Columbia, South Carolina. She currently resides in Pineville-Charlotte, North Carolina. Ms. Myers is an Entrepreneur, Humanitarian-Philanthropy, Author, Spoken Word Artist, Poet, Mentor, Purpose Coach, and a Volunteer Ambassador in several local Communities. Ms. Myers is very passionate about her skills and craft.

She continues to prevail in her journey by using life experiences and poetry writing as a therapeutic outlet to feel liberated. During her free time, she practices Spiritual Sabbatical Cleansings that pertains to Holistic Self-Maintenance, Self-Love, and Care.

BUT I LOVE YOU!

I Love You because you are valuable.

I Love You and you are worth of a healthy relationship.

I Love You and you don't have to settle.

I Love You because you deserve to loved.

I Love You because you are uniquely you.

Tammy Nobles

Tammy Nobles is the passionate founder and CEO of Tammy R. Nobles - Noble Necessities, LLC, a premier empowerment and development company. She has inspired and helped others live life intentionally through her ministry, success coaching, and leadership workshops. Tammy is a licensed Minister, and she believes in the power of positivity. She consistently inspires the world through her quotes tagged as #makeitaNOBLEday, her broadcasts known as T.E.A. with Tammy, and her Winning (WINS) day declarations. She is also the author of he *Noble Life Activity Journal*, which provides strategies to help you engineer the life you desire to live. Her favorite quote comes from the Bible: "I can do ALL things through Christ who strengthens me." Philippians 4:13.

Connect with Tammy R. Nobles via her website at TammyRNobles.com or email her at tammy@tammynobles.com.

Aftermath

She often wore dark shades.

She would take them off as the bruises would fade.

He would beat her even if she put on the wrong outfit.

Each time he promised not to hit her again, did he forget?

In her mind she knew he was wrong.

But after the beatings he would send flowers and play her favorite love songs.

And Each and every time she fell for his games.

But he was a woman beater whom only God could tame.

He beat her and made her feel like she was not worth a damn.

He called her out her name continuously and told her, "You are mines"!

The last hit left her with blood dripping from a knife.

She was supposed to be his Queen, he chose her to be his wife.

A pool of blood fills the rug.

This was not a crime committed while on drugs.

As he laid there, he thinks about all the times he has battered her beautiful face.

He regrets not walking away giving her space.

She never reported the beatings because she believed he would stop.

Now this sister is being carried away in handcuffs by the cops.

No record of the beatings just the bruised heart with the pain inside.

She took a turn down the wrong road, now she's in for a long ride.

This sister had been through a lot and she had enough.

But because she did not report it, her case was looking rough.

She was sentenced to life in prison.

She could have left him but staying was her worst decision.

Jacqueline Renee Gonder

Jacqueline Gonder is a native of Augusta, Georgia. Jacqueline has a passion for poetry and has been writing since the age of 14. After witnessing a childhood friend get killed in a drive-by at the age of 14, writing became her outlet. Jacqueline is also known as Tru the Poet. Domestic Violence is a subject near and dear to her heart. Growing up she has seen and also endured Domestic Violence firsthand. Jacqueline is currently pursuing a Master's of Science in Forensic Psychology with a specialty in Victimology. She will advocate for victims of all crimes and aid in their healing process.

The Color of Love

I just wanted to be loved, but doesn't everyone?
Did I settle, just because I wanted a man?
I got a ring, so I thought I won.
The ring is on my eye, but you don't understand.
You are telling me this, but I'm feeling like that.
What do you know about love? He loves me.
You are telling me I got to move one, but he's frat.
But with him is where I want to be.
I want to leave; I really do!
I'm not as strong as you. I'm not you!
I am strong too.
My love is red, not black, and blue.

LeDesma "Desi" Terry

LeDesma "Desi" Terry is a native of Chicago, Illinois. She is married with two children and currently resides in Elgin, South Carolina. Desi is the proud owner of Desi Therapy. As a retired Army Officer, LeDesma has served in the human service, food service, and logistical fields. She has a host of assignments to put under her belt, including "Operations Iraq Freedom", 2nd Infantry Division, South Korean, 101st Air Assault, and 3rd Infantry Division Rock of the Marne. Her education includes a Master of Arts, Liberty University; Bachelors of Science, Northern Michigan University; Southeastern Esthetics Institute: Licensed, The Nail School of Manicuring, Southeastern Institute; and Licensed Bodywork and Massage Therapist.

Learned Behavior

Big red lips...

Cheek bones bared this blush

Eyeshadow laid on sorta heavy, seemingly by a set of heavy hands

Her I.G. caption read:

"Face beat by... boyfriend" ... who wasn't a make-up artist

Well, he was sort of a make-up artist

He would make up arguments to justify his violence

Every song sad, like a violin

House a horrid choir, and he was the lead singer

He'd lead with a bunch of blues infused apologies and she would cry off key in the background

A dysfunctional duet, she wanted to leave him but wouldn't do it

Wouldn't fair well with family and friends who were unaware of their family affairs.

Didn't wanna ruin the Huxtable like image

She didn't know how to explain that Mr. Huxtable was spiking her face with abuse, so she spent most of her days in a daze, punch drunk

When in public, every smile hurt like pulling teeth

His public image was polished like new shoes so the world worshipped the ground he walked on

They didn't know the same hand he waved with had a special way of cutting off her airway

She'd get choked for swallowing too loud, so when he was in a rage she tried to ease away while saving her spit

Paranoid that he'd use a pair of fist to assist her with sleeping

Their two young boys would watch the abuse like boxing on Pay-per-view

When the winner was thru, he'd tell his opponent, " I love you"

So when these youngsters grow up and find love, what do you think they're gonna do?

Obbie West

Edward Wilson, a.k.a. Obbie West is the owner of Words of West, LLC and is an international spoken word artist, advocate, and author. Originally from Los Angeles, California. Edward is a retiree from the United States Army. He began writing in 2011 and later published his first acclaimed book of poetry entitled "Blossom."

He travels the world as an educator, trainer, and speaker using poetry to tackle tough topics such as sexual violence, prevention, and awareness. Edward has invested a personal and sincere interest in shifting the climate around sexual assault and harassment throughout the U.S. Military, universities, and communities at large.

Sexual Assault
There's Nothing Inspirational About Rape

"You have to be grateful," people tell me,
"Your experience made you who you are today
write something inspiring if you're going to write about rape."

"Isn't the first rule of writing
write what you know?" I reply.
"I write poems of my life
about my first, second and third rapes
horrible and terrifying at only fourteen."

"No," my mother says, "you didn't count
the time when you were nine."

"Like much of my past,
I must have blocked it out."

My mother adds "or that time
when you were four."

What sick freak rapes a child at four??

This I know………… THIS is all I know
I am a fighter and a survivor
rape should be talked about
exploited for what it is
an act of power, control, and violence
but there is nothing inspirational about it

I am not grateful it happened
I could have been so much better
without
 the experience
the suicidal aftermath
 the nightmares and flashbacks
 the constant hyper-vigilance

and trying to live ignoring
the fear of it happening again
because for me, apparently, it does

rape didn't make me who I am today
I chose to take another breath
I chose to hold on a bit longer
I spent the time to reinvent my life
I did that! Me.

Rape is not inspiring
it only took from me

I will not be grateful for lessons
no one should ever have to learn
Rape didn't teach me anything
I taught myself to survive

And I will write about it anyway I like.

Hear Me

Less valued than a penny at the bottom of a well
love and trust turned to bitterness and anger
a beautiful life turned into a living hell

cast in a world of consequences
for something I never wanted
forgetting I owned the key

feeling such a deep wound
as the protective layers unveil
what they fought so hard to maintain
secrets come to light

a million feelings crashing down
pools of tears
wanting to run away
from myself

hoping for a better past
while battling depression and fear
a game that can't be won
the struggle continues
refusing to stay down
overcoming again and again
false realities shatter

dark dependencies
are forever broken

finding the way out
being a light for others
saying the words
deeply moving, stories of survival

now empowered
with strength and words
speaking my truth

You will hear me

AmyAnna Soto

AmyAnna Soto is a dynamic public speaker, artist, and poet. She is a survivor of childhood sexual abuse, rape, and stalking. By being a group leader, she found her strengths in inspiring, supporting and advocating for others. AmyAnna served on the board of a nonprofit addressing dissociative disorders. She co-coordinated an annual conference for dissociative disorders and also a child abuse survivor speak out event. Currently AmyAnna is a participant coordinator for a nonprofit focused on helping others recover from traumatic experiences. She is also a co-host to a blogtalk radio show that gives survivors of sexual abuse a platform to tell their stories. AmyAnna has published one poetry book and is writing her memoir. Her passion is encouraging others to heal adverse life experiences through art and creative writing.

Betrayed

You made me smile
You made me feel loved and wanted
You told me you wouldn't hurt me
You told me I could trust you
The one thing I wanted to keep
We fought about it
You tricked me into believing you
You said you were sorry and you weren't
It started out innocent till it wasn't
I told you get off me please I don't want to
You said you have teased me long enough
You took the one thing I held closest to me my virginity
Then you disappeared
But your name and face are forever etched into my brain

Sarah Vanalstyne

This was written from the eyes of a 16-year-old girl who had already been through so much and ended up hurt by yet another person she trusted. I am 33 years old now and a mom to two wonderful girls and all I can do is hope they don't go through the same thing as I did. This was a poem written by a girl detailing a rape when I was 16, by my then boyfriend. I was a virgin and had planned on staying one till I met the right one.

My Inception

Brought into a world by force, threat, and intimidation,
Is how I came to be,
Wandering and hopelessly searching
For the sperm that created me…

Little did I know that my search
Would come back null and void
For he had no intentions of sticking around to be my Daddy
The day he took my mother's joy…

But instead she carried this baby
She never asked to have
And gave me the best life she could
Yet I still find myself oh so sad…

I'm sad and angry
That I may be a constant reflection of my mother's pain
A hurt that she should have never should have endured
As she tried to find her smile again…
But Will She Ever?

Scharnelle L. Hamlin

Scharnelle L. Hamlin is a native of Surry County, Virginia. Ms. Hamlin is a veteran of United States Air Force where she served as a Security Forces Member. After receiving an Honorable Discharge from the Air Force, Scharnelle attended Old Dominion University where she received her Bachelor of Science Degree in Human Services, Liberty University, earning her Master of Arts Degree in Professional Counseling, but her greatest honor came June 29, 2013, when she was deemed The Outstanding Graduate at Strayer University for maintaining a 4.0 GPA while perusing her second Master's degree in Education with an Adult Development Concentration.

Today, Scharnelle works as the Director for Surry County Victim Witness Assistance Program and a NOVA Crisis Responder for the Eastern Region. In her spare time, Scharnelle coaches Varsity Volleyball for her High School and is an avid volleyball and softball player. She is the proud mother of two sons, Ja'Khi and Christian and the daughter of Jeanette Taylor.

Sleepless: The Invisible Scar No One Can See

It's one of the hottest days of the summer, nighttime comes soon. Did you know scars can be painful? I do.

Some scars are better left unseen. I've kept mine hidden for years. I put on a smile as if it was makeup trying to hide them.

But just like a soda. When my body tries to fall asleep, and my mind relaxes like a coke cola bottle that's been shook; the contents shoot out vivid details in my dreams it seems... Wait, shouldn't dreams be pleasant?

As a child, do you remember before going to sleep your mom saying, "pleasant dreams"? Well, my "unpleasant dreams" became screams and I scream awaken by the nightmares. I've relived my reality for decades as my mind and body keeps the score. I lay awake sleepless once more.

Left with the remnants of stained panties and pain "down there." I was 13. I awoke groggy, feeling pain from forced entry into my womb. Now I could never offer my virginity to my future groom. Stolen was my power and ability to consciously and freely give my consent. In a daze and not quite sure why it had happened to me. I'm somehow imprisoned to this reality.

Afraid that I would not be believed but blamed so I blamed me. I was only a child. A child forced by fear to live my reality in silence. I felt powerless and dirty. He was an adult, who would believe me? My innocence shattered and my silence gave wings for the perpetrator to escape like a thief. Now I'm afraid to fall asleep. My mind on replay wondering would it have happened if I was awake? Would he still enter my room, and enter my womb? Thoughts crowd my mind and I watch time go by too scared to sleep, I count sheep. Now it's daylight and I still can't sleep.

Ashamed, I blamed me, fear silenced me, and I felt guilty for having a developing body. Now scarred and sleepless I lay awake watching the door, listening to the nighttime noise that doesn't lull me, still sleepless. God please just, make it go away, I cried silently.

As the days become weeks; the weeks become months and the months become years. The tears kept coming and now I am 23. Footloose and fancy free, I am in the military. You see now I thought I was skilled to protect me, no one would ever again hurt me. Little did I know… not all military personnel could be trusted as I had become accustomed to. Unforeseen, I failed to see, that his hidden agenda was my destiny.

Summer months use to be my favorite now it's just another trigger, that goes off like my 9-millimeter. Then it happened again. This time I was sleepwalking, not really but I must have been or why didn't I see what was about to happen? His weapon of choice was a friendly demeanor, I was caught off guard and weaponless. His fist slammed into my hand, and my keys flew down the hall into darkness. Before I could formulate a question WHY… I felt the air being choked from my windpipes as I was dragged and slammed onto a bed. My hands trying to fight for freedom. He yells out…DON'T MOVE or else. God, please let me wake up from this nightmare but when I open my eyes he is still there. I'm struggling to breathe and scared to move. I begged for my life as quiet tears fall. His response was a gun put to my head. I waited for what seemed like hours as he continued to rape me. I always thought that I would die fighting, but I laid there praying he would let me live to raise my little girl. So, I kept quiet. The uncertainty if I would live to hold my daughter again had me frozen in place, tears stained my face. Thoughts of my daughter growing up without me, I couldn't fathom, so I lay there my will broke. I wanted to live for my little girl you see. I needed to ensure this would not be her destiny. I denied my body the ability to move or breathe; my chest tightens, I struggle to catch breathe, I look into the eyes of a stranger who I once thought was a safe friend. His face and voice still haunt me when I close my eyes. Shallow breathing and… I blank out.

A Survivor:

Did you know? A scar is defined as a mark left on the skin or within the body after wounds heal from physical injury or surgery. Well, what about the mind? Can it be scarred? Thoughts crowd my mind and I watch time go by still too scared to sleep, I count sheep. Now it's daylight and I still can't sleep. Wait is this a repeat. Am I dead or alive? Reality tugs at my throat by hands that remind me that I was not dreaming. He released me and I ran for my life not looking back just in case he changed his mind. If I die, I will die running; running towards freedom and what will eventually become my new normal. But my life really isn't as normal as it might appear, I'm just existing. As the sting from the painful scars remind me of what was but feels like is and when I dream, I can't distinguish between what the past and the present is. My body keeps the score and my mind the triggers.

It is one of the hottest days of the summer; nighttime comes soon and I'm sleepless... so I hid behind the four walls of my room with locked doors searching for my new normal, while the invisible scars no one can see waits.

Tara Rivers

Tara Rivers is a poet. Poetry has been part of her therapy for years. When she became an adult, she realized writing poetry was therapeutic for her. Tara is a survivor and very passionate about helping others. In 2016 she completed the required training through the Department of Defense Sexual Assault Advocate Certification Program (D-SAACP) and serves as a credentialed Sexual Assault Prevention & Response Victim Advocate (SAPR-VA) in the military. Tara has served over 32 years and currently still serving. She has four adult children.

Can You Hear Me Now??

What do I have to do for you to hear my cry?

What will it take for you to really listen and actually give a damn?

You say you care; you say you will work on doing better but you never do.

I'm over trying to get you to hear my pain, my hurt, my voice period.

I've tried sitting down and talking.

I've ignored the problem until I couldn't anymore.

Then when I finally had enough, I blew up in anger.

Your response then is, I'm acting like a bitch, a brat, and I'm selfish, disrespectful "or you simply say

"That's Nikki being Nikki, a hot head."

I feel like I'm stuck in this world where you treat me like I'm a toddler learning to walk yet with every step I take you push me down and say aww try again while laughing at my cries.

Some say I allow it, maybe I do, maybe I did.

But no more! I have a voice that needs and will be heard.

I have something to say, rather you agree or not in what I have to say is on you.

But just know your acceptance is no longer needed or required. Nor will I allow you to define my feelings of self-worth.

I'm a smart, intelligent, strong, sexy as hell, Black woman of GOD who has a voice.

You can either get on board with this Nikki, or you can exit stage left.

Either way, I'm fine, my cries will no longer be pushed aside.

I matter. God tells me that every day he wakes me up.

I will be respected by YOU and anyone else that I grace and honor with my presence.

I love you and always will

However, it's on you now.

CAN YOU HEAR ME NOW?... BITCH!!!!

Bye Bye Nikki

There was once a girl named Nikki

Nikki to everyone one was funny the life of the party, had a heart of pure gold, with just enough sassiness to let you she had some bite in her

Nikki however funny on the outside was in pain on the inside. She was violated in so many was it really was nothing to laugh at. Her life started off by a father who abandoned her cause her mom married another man. A man who stepped up and raised her only to later abandon her for his own personal battle with his demons. He would later re-enter her life several times to walk away for selfish guilty reasons, until he walked out forever leaving her to feel more alone and abandoned than ever before.

Nikki was also violated by boys and we call them boys cause a real man would never force his self on any woman. The first sexual violation came at the age of 8 by a family member she saw often it would go on for the next 4 years. Other young family members also violated Nikki. She often blocked the incidents out. She was violated again her freshmen year in college and incident she blames herself for. She was drinking and partying with her roommates and a brother of a guy she was really crushing on. That brother would later rape her as she slept, she thought she was dreaming of having sex with the guy she was actually crushing on. But after getting a call from her roommate who informed her that he immediately got on the phone and called to brag to his brother about the chicks he FUCKED all in a 12-hour period.

Yes, he had sex with her other roommate that one was consensual the one with Nikki was not and I repeat was NOT. But in true Nikki form she never said anything she let it go and so did the possible relationship with her crush he never spoke to her again.

Nikki was also violated by people taking advantage of her kindness and huge loving heart. Many have lied, stolen, and plan mistreated her. Some would say she allowed it. Others would say the people were to blame. Nikki simply said I thought they loved me as I loved them, I guess I'm just unlovable.

Nikki was also a person who was listened to by her family. The same family who would be pissed by others who mistreated her was also guilty of doing the same exact thing it just came in a different package. Her family had their own way of living Nikki it often came off as uncaring or suffocating. You see Nikki was the oldest daughter, and granddaughter yet treated like the youngest. As she was expected to carry herself as the oldest the often treated her like a helpless child. Nikki had epilepsy and her family often use that to keep Nikki from being more independent. She lives at home she does drive but the expectation is when they needed Nikki to do something she was often never asked but told. And when she was asked No was never to be an option.

Nikki knew where he unconditional love came from the only constant in her life that was God. Which is why her one attempt to take her own life never happened. Which is also why her seizures never took her out but made her stronger. God has a purpose over her life. He wants her voice to be heard, he wants her anger/hurt/ and pain to go away so others can be blessed by her God given blessing. Nikki is changing and with that change many will not be on board and she is finally beginning to be ok with that.

Through her newfound growth and enlightenment Nikki is finally starting to see her storm going away. As that storm moves away Nikki's wings are taking off. Nikki is dying she is going home to be with God. But don't be sad for her no ma'am because although Nikki is gone Kim is still here living and walking the walk God has for her. Are you confused? Nikki was a nickname given to a little girl at birth. Kim is her God given name the name of this beautiful strong, funny woman you will forever see. So let me introduce you to Kim Nicole and let's say goodbye to Nikki. BYE BYE NIKKI!!!

Kim N. Hardy

Kim N. Hardy is a South Carolina Native who lives and works in Columbia, SC. She began having seizures at a young age and was not aware that she had epilepsy. In 2015, after many years of feeling "different" and frustrated with her diagnosis, God led her to create Hardy Handz Foundation, a 501c3 nonprofit organization that educate, inform, and support those with Epilepsy and their family. With Hardy Handz Foundation Kim realized there was an opportunity to breaking stereotypes about Epilepsy and break the silence of people suffering with Epilepsy alone.

In 2019, Kimberly wrote, Adventures of Wallee and Kimmie "Wallee to the Rescue". This is the first book in her series for children, to explain how epilepsy can affect them and their family. Kim volunteers at her church and speaks at events to raise Epilepsy Awareness.

Child Sexual Abuse
I Never Told

He told me that I was special and gave me gifts.
He told me to trust him.
He told me that it wouldn't hurt and to close my eyes.
He told me to pull my pants down so he could see my private.
He told me to open my eyes as he pulled his pants down
So I could see his private.
He told me that they are the same and should touch.
He told me that I would always be his best boy.

Best Boy

Best Boy has decided to remain anoymous, but he wanted to share his expeirence with child sexual abuse from a male's perspective. He wants all men to know that they are not alone. His faviorite quote is "Girls and boys need protecting."

I WAS

I was YOUR VICTIM
I have a FACE
I was a CHILD
Was there no DISGRACE?
You were my ABUSER
You have a NAME
You were an ADULT
Have you any SHAME

MY BODY IS MY BODY

My body is my body
It is not for your mere pleasure
When you look at me
You don't see me
You see your pleasure
You see something to have power over
To control
To take from it want you want
You don't ask you just look and you take without my permission
You look with your eyes
You undress me
You never ask yourself
How your thoughts, your actions could break me
If I knew your thoughts
If I could see your eyes
Drift down to places that are off limits to you
I would tell you how much in that moment
You just stole from me
I am not just a woman; I am a person
and,
My body is mine
Does not your body belong to you?
Do you look at your daughter that way?
Your mother that way?

Your sister?
Your aunt?
Your friend?
I do not take delight in being a source of meat; your pound of flesh to take
When your weakness is all that, you have to retreat to when you are hungry
I am filled with my own shame
My own guilt
I do not need you to fill me with yours
Stop your eyes; your mind from wandering
I am not yours
My body, my flesh is mine and mine alone…

Me Too

Someone once asked me how others could tell
That if on the inside they were living in hell
I said,
Me too!
Someone once asked me how nobody could know
Of the pain hidden within that they tried hard not to show
So I said,
Me too!
Someone once asked me how do they learn to live?
With all of the damage that somebody else did
So I said,
Me too!
Someone once asked me how I knew
That they had been damaged and broken from sexual abuse
So I said,
Me too!
Someone once asked me how It felt
too finally tell and have nobody help
So I said,
Me too!
Someone once asked me how do they do it?
Trying to go on like there's nothing to it
So I said,
Me too!
Someone once asked me how they survive

Living with all the hurt inside
So I said,
Me too!

Healing Hearts and Souls from Broken too Beautiful

Debra Monk

Debra Monk is a survivor of child sexual abuse, domestic violence, sexual assault, child porn and incest. In 2007, she started writing about her feelings after an overturned supreme court conviction of one of her abusers. Since then, many things have happened to help her towards healing and taking back her power. Every time she shares her writing's through her story, she speaks her truth. Truth is freedom, for both the giver and receiver. Debra is an advocate, social worker, veteran, wife, mother, grandmother, and author. Her personal statement: Life is and can be lived. We just have to figure out how to live it!!!

Molested

His name was Joe
He came thru the doe
And pushed me to the floe
And called me a hoe

And I said no
But he wouldn't go
So he grabs my fro
And tells me to show

And flashed me some doe
Yeah, I felt real low
But he wanted some mo
And didn't let go

Many times in a row
Then left me so
That's all I know
His name was Joe.

Jessica Lewis

Jessica Lewis is a survivor of trauma & abuse. She is stronger than her past & decided to overcome rather than be a victim. God is the head of her life & has helped her become who she is today. Jessica is a poet & activist for all human rights and equality. Her moto is "Let's make the world a better place together."

Between Sisters

I'm not saying it didn't happen.
I just don't remember that day.
What do you want me to say?
Yes, I believe you!

Why do I have to say, "he hurt me too"?
If you already know the truth.
Please, just let me be!

Yes, his voice and his smell haunt me .
This is my truth, and you have yours.
Pushing him out of my mind helps me feel free.
Choosing not to remember is my sanity.

**LaDesma Terry's biography is shared under her Domestic Violence poem.

Dancing In The Rain

Summer rains
Warm as can be
Touching my skin
Washing all over me.

Dancing in the rain
As it sets me free
Feeling my virtue
Freeing my identity.

Autumn rains
As all life fades
Into the background
Cutting short the days.

Dancing in the rain
As it sets me free
Felling my virtue
Freeing my identity.

Winter rains
In the form of snow
Buries all the sin
Covers all the sorrows.

Dancing in the rain
As it sets me free
Felling my virtue
Freeing my identity.

Spring rains
That bring forth new life
Pain is washed away
In the trickling rivers of strife.

Dancing in the rain
As a brand new me
Given a second chance
To discover what I can be.

I am someone in this world.
I am discovering life inside of me.
I am worth something,
Even if I'm the only one…who will ever see.

Serenity Carino

Serenity is a survivor of multi-generational trauma which includes psychological, mental, emotional, verbal, sexual, physical, sadistic, and financial abuses. She spent nearly her entire life in fear; and is able to trace freeze responses and anxiety attacks to pre-toddler years.

Serenity finally sought therapy and abandon her abuse two years ago and began the adventure into her healing journey. She has been diagnosed with CPTSD, Dissociative Disorders, DDNOS (mild form of DID; age shifting).

Some forms of therapy include music, art, poetry, singing lessons, crystals & energy healing, her adopted family, taking care of her four-legged kids, and a special favorite, Gracie Women Empowered Jujitsu. She gives credit to Jehovah God and believes that without God, she wouldn't be alive today.

Her personal statement: I can't change the past, but I am changing the narrative of my memories and slowly taking my power, self-respect and dignity back!

Journey to an Internal Place

Scared to reveal
The truth underneath
The shame, all-consuming
The fear, hard to breathe

The secret I'd held
From myself for so long
It needs to come out
I've got to stay strong

I shake in my boots
Will it ruin *his* life?
Or will it indeed
Salvage *my* mortal soul?

In an email
I ask him
"What if I speak out?"

Through his own fears and shame
Trepidation and dread
He says, "Do what you need . . .
I guess . . . sure, go ahead

"If it'll help you, I get it
Do what you must do
And maybe, just maybe
It could help . . . me too"

My brother, my perp
Was a victim as well
Serving his sentence
He, too, was in hell

What happened to him
He passed on to me
But he gave me two gifts:
Supporting my speaking — confirming my truths

As we worked through our pain
Via notes back-and-forth
It took thirteen years
Till we spoke voice-to-voice . . .

Of a word
Seldom heard . . .

Incest, you see,
Is a term often feared
But that does not make
The effects disappear

We live with the impacts
Every. Single. Day
Whether hidden or not
In our bodies, they stay

But with patience and work
Facing all that's taboo
We can move more toward healing
Believe me, it's true

I've gone from riddled with pain
And unable to share
To using my voice
And moving with flair

So I tell you my story
In hopes that it helps
Whether we're taking long strides
Or just baby steps

Each person's unique
My journey's my own
But I pray that we all
Find an internal place — that's safe to call home

Maria Socolof

Maria Socolof holds a MS degree in Environmental Health Sciences from the Harvard School of Public Health. For twenty-two years, she worked as an environmental health scientist, project manager, researcher, and technical writer. Then debilitating chronic pain took over her life after she ruptured a disk in her neck in 2005. She ultimately discovered that past traumas, including sibling incest, were feeding her physical pain. Acknowledging the connection between the mind and the body, and taking steps to face her past traumas, has led her on a path of authentic healing.

She is an author, speaker, and advocate for mindbody healing, trauma-and-chronic-pain connection, survivors of incest and childhood sexual abuse. She is a member of the RAINN Speakers Bureau, Incest AWARE, and the Sexual Assault Advocacy Network. Her memoir is, *The Invisible Key: Unlocking the Mystery of My Choric Pain*, created a website and blog, www.healingfromchronicpain.com, She is a mother of two, wife, and forever a gymnast-at-heart.

Innocent Souls

A people. A culture,
forever scarred,
from settlers and soldiers
that came from afar.

Stolen. Taken,
cast from their lands,
beaten, enslaved
colonized by the white man.

Children abducted,
locked away in a school,
far from their loved ones
the only life they understood.

What did they do,
that made them owe?
To be killed and buried
all alone in the cold.

What did they do,
that was ungodly, unseen?
You thought they were savages
unpure and unclean.

You cut off their hair,
made them feel dirty, ashamed,
You beat and tortured them
in Gods holy name.

Your secrets of horrors,
now exposed,
will justice be done
for 215 innocent souls?

May justice come
swift in the night,
As the voices of
survivors and families unite.

Dedicated to the first 215 unmarked graves of Indigenous children and the thousands after via residential schools.

Annalee Somerville

Annalee Somerville has been on a very long journey, but she has made it. She is a 'Being of Light' on a journey, of love and healing. She writes her poems from that space.
~~Love & Light~~

Choices

I didn't choose trauma
Trauma chose me
I was just a kid
I had no choice, you see

But…

I did choose… to go back
Fearing something worse
I also chose… not to tell
Though in my head I would rehearse

I chose to fight
To stay alive
I chose to give in
In order to survive

I chose to push down
My pain, I chose to avoid
And deep inside, I became
So angry and annoyed

It was time to make another choice
This time, a choice for me
I am not my trauma, and
My trauma is not me

It has controlled my life
For far too very long
It is finally time
I start to move on

I'm choosing to talk
To take down this wall
Telling MY truth
Holding back nothing at all

I'm choosing to trust
Even ask for help
As hard as it is
I'm bettering myself

I didn't choose my trauma
My trauma chose me
But I refuse to let me trauma
Keep getting the best of me.

Nikki Kelly

At 17, Nikki had enough, it was finally time to come forward. Secrets that she had been keeping for years, she finally had the strength to release. She struggled with what to say, how to tell and who, but ultimately knew what she needed to do. She gathered everything she possibly could, afraid she wouldn't be believed, and went to the police to make a report.

While her friends sat in High School Government, she sat in a courtroom learning firsthand about the law. She may not know who was crowned king or queen that year, but she will never forget the pride she had, getting justice for her violent sexual assault.

Nikki is a "tomboy," fun-loving, outgoing, and always laughing, joking, and smiling. As well as a USN Seabee disabled Veteran, with a degree in interpreting for the hearing impaired. She lives in Michigan with her husband of 26 years and two adult daughters.

Warning Signs for Parents

Changes in behavior provide possible warning signs that a child is being or has been sexually abused. Keep in mind that if your child exhibits one of these behaviors, it doesn't necessarily mean that your child is or has been abused. However, if they are exhibiting multiple signs or behaving in a manner that is inappropriate or causing you concern, we encourage you to talk to your child and seek professional help, if necessary.

- Behavior changes and outbursts
- Mood changes – withdrawn, depressed, angry, or anxious
- Attitudinal changes towards specific people
- No appetite
- An excessive layering of clothing especially in warm weather
- Bed wetting
- Acting out sexually and/or have an inappropriate level of knowledge about sex for their age
- Promiscuity
- Nightmares

- Genital issues – tearing, bleeding, odor, swelling, or STIs
- Running away (prevalent with older kids)
- Pregnancy
- Alcohol and substance abuse
- Fearing or avoiding affection

Sexual Harassment
Unemployed

Every day, I had to endure:
your piercing eyes going up and down my body,
your tongue licking your lips when I walk by,
unwelcomed comments about my skin and clothing,
your laughter and snickering,
the smell of your cologne, when you came near me,
the constant invites to dinner,
and your smile when I said NO

Finally, I reported you to our supervisor. His interrogation
and responses:
Did he touch you?
Did he hurt you?

Are you sure he wasn't just being nice?
Did you do anything to make turn him on?
Do you want him to lose his job?
What is it that you want me to do?

My response:
I QUIT.

Penetration

One joke, two jokes, now you keep staring at me.

One dinner invite. Two movie invites. Five lunch invites.

Gently brushing up against my arm, causing no physical harm.

Your eyes tell a story that I don't want to hear.

Your lips say words that created fear.

No physical penetration, but you penetrated my soul.

Amber

Amber is a Financial Officer, at a top Fortune 500 company. Her experience in Corporate America includes experiencing years of sexual harassment. She hopes that her poetry will change the outlook of sexual harassment in our society and Corporate America.

Human Trafficking Before It Had a Name

Before the term "human trafficking" existed

We still did.

It was always there, there wasn't the knowledge, awareness, and statistics.

It was right there- but time and time again, they just missed it.

Some of us tried to tell them but they dismissed it,

And how could we accurately describe it when there was no definition?

How could we begin to heal in this hopeless situation?

Before they had a label to call it what it was, we were labeled troublemakers and crazy because we resisted.

And so, we learned to be submissive, and this is how we were conditioned.

Even if we tried to speak out, no one would listen.

Stuck in a victim mentality because even after each fatality they refused to accept that she WAS the victim,

So, she tried desperately to get them to see even if it took blatant and extreme self sabotaging because after she couldn't beat them, the option left was to work with them.

But she was pushed and pushed and pushed,

And shushed and shushed and shushed.

Before the term human trafficking was known

No compassion for those trapped in the game was shown.

Victim blaming and stripper shaming was all we heard,

And its still his against her word.

Stigmatized and dehumanized, stripped of power by strip club cowards-

And she was labelled troubled and disturbed.

Before they knew what human trafficking looked like she was labelled a criminal.

They called it solicitation or public intoxication or because she didn't have an adult entertainment licence, she was put in a cell.

Even though she was a teenager, event though she was injured, or her behaviour was pain turned inward or she was being controlled and sold-

She was labelled a criminal

And those hurting her got away with it all or the consequences were minimal.

Because the system works against the victim and many of the laws written are hypocritical-

And she was labelled crazy and difficult and cynical.

Before human trafficking was spoken about,

One by one a new victim was turned out

And we fell for their tricks because we didn't know the warning signs.

We truly thought we could get ahead but ended up so far behind-

And they… just left us there.

And we were labelled as "damaged beyond repair."

Before the police understood human trafficking was common,

My mom called them!

And she warned of the signs as she saw them.

She pleaded with them that there was a problem.

They told her, next time I was out passed curfew, she had doors for a reason- lock them!

But she knew there are so many cases of missing and murdered women and children, and this is NOT how we solve them.

And she was labelled as paranoid and overprotective.

But she never gave up on me and always kept the door open for me because they were wrong-

We know it now and she knew it then.

But this was where we were. I'm alive and I survived not because of the police but because of HER.

She called them for help but that's not what she would get-

And they are labeled as those who serve and protect.

Before they knew what human trafficking looked like, they could sleep at night

While we walked the streets or worked the stage, bruised and broken in heels too tight.

As long as it wasn't their kid it was all right.

And the odds were against her because she was alone in the fight.

Now that you know what human trafficking looks like,

You can't look the other way and you can't play blind.

It's now a conscious choice if you do nothing and leave us behind.

We must stop blaming the victim, we must stand with them.

The laws and the system need to protect the victims-

Even if they need to be rewritten.

Now that you know what a victim of human trafficking looks like,

Validate her struggle- Hear her, see her,

Lend a hand or join the fight.

Stand by her. Shame the sex buyer.

Flames of toxic masculinity and patriarchy spread like wildfire.

Fires spread rapid and its proof everything is connected.

Now that you know what human trafficking is – that it is real and it exists,

Help end it.

The Game

The way it was portrayed to me by a much older man who preyed on me was so much different than how it would be.

He was a friend of my fathers and offered me protection and a place to stay when I was in need, because I was already fleeing domestic violence as a teen.

The way "the game" was portrayed to me was just that – fun and games.

I just wish I had of taken a step back or that there was someone to say to me, "Go down that path and your life will never be the same".

But I kept it a secret from the only ones who cared about me because I was ashamed.

It was portrayed to me as bright lights and fun nights.

It was portrayed to me as sexy – and sexy is what settler's society told me I needed to be.

It was a job that didn't require a degree or even I.D and coming from intergenerational poverty, that appealed to me.

"Easy and quick money" they said.

Sleazy- he was greedy, and I remained needy instead.

I would never see that money, but he was *more* than well fed.

It wasn't how it was portrayed to me.

He recruited me and groomed me and betrayed me.

But how it really was- will always stay with me.

Dark, dirty places, rooms full of ruined souls, where they only see our bodies, not our faces.

Years, and years, and years of my life wasted.

I was a slave to so many men and any kindness was pretend, they were all full of hatred.

Dirty hands all over me, dirty man's breath on me and I wished death on me, as I prayed to be free.

Objectified, and I became desensitised as I oddly obliged.

From the bars, to the hotels, to the agencies, to the streets,

Physical and sexual violence everyday and every week.

Drugs to numb the pain, then back to the same, put a smile on my face and repeat.

Attacked, can't fight back, trapped, laughed at, trying not to snap, discarded like scrap.

Beat down and beat up, and in each town police were corrupt,

And it wasn't just what happened to me, I was helpless as another girl was beat or others disappeared never again to be seen.

I was helpless and I felt like this every single day.

I felt like this and learned helplessness is part of why we stay.

So many of us wanted out, we just needed to be shown a way.

Angel Power

Angel Power is the author of "The Darkness & The Light," a peer support worker, public speaker and on a poverty reduction strategic team for a major city. She uses her lived experience to expose systemic injustices, promote change and inspire those who were silenced to use their voices. Angel's passion for advocacy stemmed from falling through cracks countless times. She refers to her initial repeat victimization, the secondary victimization, and what she calls "residual victimization" that she continues to face even today. She is also a self-healer and has turned to her spirituality to cope and to grow.

Advice to young girls and boys:

1. Don't trust anyone that makes you feel uncomfortable or touches you in your private spots.

2. Don't trust any adult, that you have to lie to your parents to be around.

3. When your gut tells you that something is wrong, believe it, and get out of the situation safely.

4. Don't think that you are untouchable and can never end up in the sex trafficking community.

5. Learn all you can learn about predators and sex trafficking. The more you know, the less likely you will become a victim.

Advice to parents:

1. Talk to your children about sex and predators at an early age.
2. Don't tell your children that you will kill anyone that hurts them because they will be scared to tell.
3. Don't trust anyone around your kids, this includes teachers, coaches, priest, pastors, neighbors, etc.
4. Always pop up unannounced if your children are spending time away from you.
5. Encourage a trusting relationship with a family or friend that you trust who your child can talk to about anything. We never told our parents everything; don't expect your children to tell you everything.
6. Don't underestimate a predator. They can ham your children.
7. Be vigilant, become informed, and attend local community events.

Dr. Guyton's Right to Tell It
R. Kelly vs. India Arie

What is your favorite R Kelly song or CD?

Most people love his music and know every beat.

Not me...because when I hear his voice, I remember the day when you asked me to go to dinner and treated me like a queen.

You were so nice, and I didn't think you could ever be evil. That is why I trusted you when you said, "Let's go to my room to watch a movie."

Your dark arms turned into snakes as they started to explore my body.

They were strong and overpowered my small hands.

Your couch turned into a bed as you pushed me down.

You took your pants down, faster than a speed of light.

I couldn't believe that you were entering my treasure, for only your pleasure.

I just laid there, with questions running through my head. Why are you doing this? Why are you hurting me? Are you wearing a condom? Will I catch AIDS? Will I get pregnant? Will you ever stop? I became lost in my thoughts as you took over my body without permission. I just laid there not fighting back with salty tears falling down my face. It was like you were running a race.

When I tuned out your heavy breathing, all I could hear was *"I don't see nothing wrong with a little bump n grind"* *"Homie Lover Friend"*

"It seems like you're ready" *"Sex me,"* and finally

"12 Play."

You raped me for the entire CD, as if it was your theme song and hours long.

So yes, I hate the sound of R Kelly's voice and the sound of your voice as you said, *"Soldier, no one will believe you."*

Now I am healing, and I use my voice to help others to escape the demise of rape. Today, my tears still fall, but they are full joy as they flutter down my face like beautiful butterflies.

Your actions no longer have me bound so I no longer frown.

I have replaced R Kelly with India Arie.

"Life is a Journey, Not a Destination there are no mistakes just chances were taking,"

"It's a Beautiful Day", "I Am Light" and *"Now I am Ready for Love."*

And ready to conquer the shame by placing it on you because you should be ashamed of what you did to me.

You were wrong. They believe me and instead of fighting a war in Iraq, I leave the battle to God who has my back.

Private Vanessa Dunn (Guyton)

*This poem was written to allow myself to heal and to stop my mind from racing. I added to this poem to reflect my healing.

After Trauma vs. After Healing

My hair, my smile, my breast, are all fake. They are purposeful because they cover the sadness in my life. They hide my fears, my insecurities , and mistakes. Only few ever get to see the real me. She is protected in a cocoon from the harmful environment.

Hopefully one day the butterfly will appear but until then the FAKE ME shall remain and sustain.

Drumroll!!!!

My hair is natural, my smile is bright, my eyes light up… genuinely.

This is purposeful because now I exude the joy of unleashing my shame to heal.

I no longer hide my fears and insecurities.

I no longer and blame myself for the actions of the man who violated me.

Now, everyone is allowed to see the REAL Me.

The cocoon slowly opened after therapy and spiritual work, to reveal a beautiful and vibrant butterfly. My colors are vibrant, and my wingspan reaches others who are stuck in their cocoon due to trauma.

No longer will I hide my story. Instead I will share, as I soar all around the world.

Antidepressant Medication

Pills, Pills, Pills

Prescribed to remove my suicidal thoughts and cure my ills.

I hate taking these various colors.

Because temporarily I feel like another.

Time slows down, but my frown slowly turns upside down.

When it gets in my system, I feel less pain.

I no longer have tears flowing like rain or feel insane.

I can remove my mask, which before was a hard task.

Latrice disappears and allow Vanessa to reappear.

Some may say I am crazy because I take pills, but I say I am crazy for not taking meds that bring back thrills.

Today, I am proud to say, that medication is why I am living today.

Butterfly Freedom

I want the butterflies to stop by.

Because I am amazed that beauty can fly.

I admire how they transform from a cocoon then freely bloom.

I admire how they are free.

Free to be an individual that is different like me.

***Dedicated** to all victims being held captive.

Sexual Slaves-A Perspective From My Ancestors

Imagine a wooden boat, floating in an ocean of beautiful blue water. You can hear the waves but can never see them because you are chained in the bottom of this vessel. Hot, sweaty, hungry, and lying in your own feces. The journey takes months, but you survive to step on newfound land.

Slavery captured my ancestors physically and mentally.

They were raped, beaten, lynched, castrated, forced into incest, and raped again.

Husbands were forced to rape other women to reproduce a child born into slavery as property.

Wives were forced to make love to Master and have his mixed breed children, only to be hated by the Misses.

The children who were consumed through rape were sold and never seen again.

Brothers and sisters were forced to have sex in front of master and his company for humor and entertainment.

Men were raped by poachers to emasculate them and remove their pride so they never run and hide again.

The Misses was just as bad. She had her choice of Black men on the plantation who she forced to satisfy her. At times for her own pleasure, and other times as revenge because she knew mister had his fun.

This epidemic has not stopped. The secret continues and the results are seen in our culture and families.

Do not try to act like it didn't happen and silence or ignore the abuse.

Do not act like you can't understand the separation and hatred seen in our culture.

Do not act like you can't see how we are still getting fucked in society by master and the misses, who are still the bosses in organizations and who still pay us less than our counterparts with less experience and education.

Don't act like you can't see the self-hatred of our bodies, hair, and skin color by some of us.

Don't act like you don't see how we are still imprisoned at higher rates and receive more prison time for similar crimes of white criminals. Not to mention the high rates of our people who have been found innocent due to DNA and withheld evidence.

Trauma passes through generations in many forms to include domestic violence. The pain of slavery has not been erased or properly addressed in our society.

Will you take a stand with us and speak against these injustices? It is time for us to stop getting raped over and over again?

Imprisoned, wagon trains, boats, horseback, tree hangings, cross burnings.

Beatings lead to more beatings which is domestic violence. It is a sickness that needs to be healed.

Rise with us to **HUSH No More**.

Signed our Ancestors

Heartbreak & Rebirth

The lies and adultery sliced my heart into miniature pieces, leaving no hope in sight.

Heartbreak took my heartbeat and faith in love away like a thief in the night.

I was so crushed that I asked God "Was that right?"

My dreams shattered, my strength disappeared, my eyes darkened, and my soul dried up.

The only thing remained was my fake smile and of course my strut.

I was dead from the inside out. I was so broken I could no longer argue or shout.

One day, my spiritual advisor appeared, and I was told to "live and love again."

I was so scared of the thought of me opening up my heart, just to be mistreated and mentally abused.

The idea of Live and Learn had me very confused.

I stood in the mirror and said to myself "Rebirth is required for you to live your life, to experience pure joy and happiness without strife."

At that moment, I forgave, so I could be reborn and no longer mourn.

The butterfly appeared out of her cocoon, flying and dancing around the room.

She experienced a beautiful rebirth from the inside out. She was so full of self-happiness, that she no longer had to argue and shout.

Her smile and eyes regained their color. Even the possibility returned to love another.

She realized that after her heartbreak. She had to take a break, to dissolve the spiritual ache.

She also realized that her life was destined for greatness and needed color, in the form of true love from another.

Falling In Love Again

After years of protecting my heart and not believing in love; I've met someone who makes me feel like I am floating above.

Floating above the pain, hurt and strife, which is interesting because it's changing my life.

I never thought I would love anymore; but his spirit has opened the door.

I feel like a giddy girl; like the first time a cute boy rocked my world.

I am smiling from ear to ear, like I want to do a high school cheer.

I hope he values the journey we are about to embark; and gently handles my heart.

I am going to experience "Falling in Love Again," surrendering my heart and creating a new start.

*Dedicated to Survivors. There is hope.

Dr. Vanessa Dunn Guyton

Dr. Vanessa Dunn Guyton is a Survivor of Military Sexual Trauma (MST) who is also a champion for Victims and Survivors all over the world. In 2017, she started her healing journey after remembering her sexual assault. She used poetry, as a way to express her feelings and to document her roller coaster of emotions. Today, she continues to work on her spiritual relationship with God, and uses natural healing modalities to remain sober, elevate, and heal. Dr. Guyton enjoys learning, eating good food, visiting beaches, and traveling all around the world to experience various cultures. Contact her on social media or email her at vguyton@hushnomore.org for speaking engagements and training.

Support/ Words of Encouragement

After experiencing trauma, we must remember that our lives are not over. For this reason, we all need to find a healthy way to adopt a lifestyle that includes progress, growth, and elevation. One of the hardest things to do is to live a healthy lifestyle that includes exercise, sleep, good eating habits, spiritual practices, and emotional well-being. Finding the courage to motivate and encourage ourselves, during those difficult times, is part of living a healthy life. Research has shown that speaking positive words to yourself, on a daily basis, can improve your mood, improve your interactions with others, and increase your overall outlook on life. Below is an affirmation that you can use to include positivity in your life and to prevent those negative ideas from consuming your mind. Always remember that

YOU ARE NOT YOUR TRAUMA; YOU ARE A SURVIVOR. YOU HAVE A RIGHT TO HEAL.

My Daily Affirmation

I AM Smart.

I AM Kind.

I AM Beautiful.

I AM Important.

I AM Talented.

I AM the Leader of MY Family.

Written for me by my amazing daughter, Teaira. Our children are full of wisdom, and can help us heal.

Teaira Mack

Teaira Mack is the Founder and conduit of Rooted Vibrationz, a Holistic Healing Studio located in Columbia/Cayce, SC. She is a gifted Intuitive Herbalist, Certified Reiki practitioner and Meditation teacher. She specializes in energy healing, shadow work, herbalism, candle magik, mindful meditation, crystal energy and so much more. Teaira was born into a very spiritually gifted family and began diving deeper into my Spiritual journey and Holistic wellness in 2018. Her role is to assist Victim Advocates in effectively integrating mindfulness and holistic wellness to help victims and survivors overcome trauma. Teaira services, led to her being awarded the 2022 "Women in Rising" award. Visit https://linktr.ee/Rootedvibrationz for more information or to book a Consultation to explore healing options.

Better Days

Better days are waiting for you

That will help you to forget about your blues

As the pain in your heart slowly fades

And the frown on your face slowly turns into a smile

You finally have decided to take a stand.

As you follow your heart and accepting God's Master Plan.

Better days remind you of how sweet life can be.

When you surrender your pain and fear to become free.

I AM

I am unique, powerful, and blessed,

For God created me in His Glorious Image.

He believes that I will achieve my destiny,

No matter what others may think of me.

God has given me the knowledge and strength,

To accept and embrace the wonderful child that I am.

For His Love protects me, even though you may doubt it.

For God's love reminds me to lift my head and smile.

Even when my fears cause my heart to skip a beat, when

I am going through life's trials to become who I am supposed to be.

I am beautiful even though my lips may speak of past hurts and fears.

I am strong even when my mind may reflect on pass hurts and pains,

That I thought I had forgotten as I attempted to bury them over the years.

I am more than you will ever know because one day He saw me and felt my pain.

The Father gently began to speak life into my inner being.

As He daily began to caress my soul and orchestrate my healing.

That gave me a peace that calmed the rage within me.

As God's love and patience began to empower me.

Challenging me to embrace the awesome wonderful me that He created.

Friends

Friends may come and go.

But of one thing you can be sure of…

If you don't love, respect, and take care of yourself,

How can you expect anyone else to?

Trouble don't last always

And pain will surely go away.

If you keep yourself in good health,

And stay out of the other person's way,

Long life can be yours.

Even though ups and downs will occur.

Yet, you can handle them all with daily prayer.

You Are

You are more than a statistic from a group of haters.

You are more than the roadblocks placed in your path.

You are here to change lies into truth.

You are here to achieve a divine purpose.

You are here to remind others that they are God's Glory here on earth.

You are here to witness, live, and tell the Redemption Story.

You are here to win the battle against prejudice.

You are here to share the Good News with mankind.

You are here to tell the truth in the good and bad times.

You are here to receive God's ordained success and favor.

You are here to challenge yourself to excel and walk in God's Divine Purpose for you.

Lord

Lord, I feel your blessings,

They are flowing all around.

I feel them in my heart,

Like a gentle breeze that blows.

Caressing and nurturing me when I am weak.

Giving me the strength, I will need to survive.

Lord, I feel your miracles, on a beautiful day,

As the wind blows gently,

Like a mother rocking her baby as she sings a lullaby.

Soothing her baby until it drifts off to sleep.

Lord, I feel your peace, as it wakes me every day.

Calming me in times of distress and rage

Even when I forget to pray.

Robin D. Whitehead Rudolph

Robin Denise Whitehead-Rudolph is a mother and grandmother. She is an ordained minister, teacher of the word of God, conference speaker, lyrics writer, playwright, and singer. She is the owner of "Created For Me By You"; which is a platform for spiritual writings that includes plays and training for religious education and photography.

She has several closed pages on Facebook (Delicate Love, Nothing But The Truth Study and Mentee Training). The purpose is to bless those who want to learn and heal without unnecessary distractions.

She has several degrees (MS in Performance Improvement (with distinctions), a Bachelor in Business Management (Cum Laude), and several Associates in Education, Business and Religion.

What to Consider After Experiencing a HUSH Topic?

After experiencing a traumatic event, you may feel overwhelmed, and feel like your thoughts are consumed with the event. Below are steps that you can consider, to help you transition from Victim to Survivor.

1. Safety is the most important thing you should focus on. Consider calling 9-1-1, family member/friends, or a local advocacy agency to report the incident. Local police officers, victim advocates, and counselors can help you develop a safety plan or help you apply for a restraining order.

2. Health is also a major concern. Consider going to your local hospital for an examination. A victim advocate can accompany you to the hospital or can be called once you get there. When you arrive at the hospital, go to the check-in desk, and tell them that you need to speak to someone in private. The hospital staff will immediately take you to the back so that you do not have to speak in front of the entire waiting room. The hospital will assign a Doctor or a Sexual Assault Nurse Examiner to examine and support you through the process.

Remember that the hospital can test you for pregnancy and sexually transmitted infections, as well as collect evidence that can be used to prosecute your offender. They hospital can also give you emergency contraception (EC). This is medication used to prevent pregnancy. This form of birth control can delay ovulation, stop fertilization of an egg, or stop an egg from attaching. EC is not an abortion and does not end an existing pregnancy.

3. Counseling is something that victims forget about because some injuries are not seen. If you are experiencing any anxiety, sleep disturbances, increase substance use, or depression, or if you are feeling suicidal, talk to your primary care doctor, counselor, or advocate. Your mental health is just as important as your physical health.

4. Healing is the ultimate step to achieve after a traumatic event. This step and timing is different for everyone. Hopefully, this book will encourage you to take the first step.

How Do I HUSH No More?

Coming forward and sharing your truth is a hard decision because it is NOT easy. When you are ready, answer these three questions. After you have fully answered these questions, add the answers into your story as you share your truth. Remember that people may not believe you or agree with your decision. During these times, remember that You Have a Right to Tell It & Heal.

1. Who am I? (You are NOT what happened to you.)
2. What have I learned? (Don't blame yourself.)
3. What do I need to do to move forward as a Survivor?

5 Ways to Prevent Sexual Abuse:

1. Become informed about the tactics that offenders use to commit abuse.
2. If you have to keep a meeting with someone a secret, don't go. Your friends and family should always know where you are and who you are with.
3. Never trust your drinks or food around anyone. Covering it up does not protect you from being

drugged. Don't let someone buy or make you a drink without you watching.

4. Say an assertive "NO" and stand your ground. Don't say "maybe" or sound unsure. Make sure you leave the situation.

5. Use your intuition. If your mind tells you not to do it, or your stomach feels queasy, pay attention. Our body has a natural safety alarm

Friends & Family Support

5 Ways to Prevent or Interrupt an Act of Violence

1. Increase awareness: Make eye contact with the victim to let them know you're aware and look for their signals. Asses the best way to step-in or if the situation is too dangerous to approach alone.

2. Distraction: Do what you can to interrupt the situation. A distraction can give someone a chance to get to a safe place. Cut off any conversation with a diversion. You can also move around physically in a way to create space that disrupts the conversation or potentially harmful behaviors.

3. Ask for help: It can be intimidating to approach a situation alone. Enlist another person to support and come with you when you approach the person at risk. You can also ask someone to intervene in your place, like a friend, bartender, or security guard.

4. Be direct: Talk directly to the person who might be in trouble. Ask questions like "Who did you come here with?" "Would you like me to stay with you?".

Once the act is under control or over, offer your support. You can be an ally by letting victims know you stand with them and finding out what they need and how can you better support them after an incident. A simple, "How are you?" "Can I do anything?" "I am sorry this happened." "I am here for you.". Positive words and offering your support can make a huge difference.

GIVE is a way that you can remember how to be supportive to your friends and family members when they come to you for help.

Gentle: Be gentle and courteous. Don't judge or blame.

Interested: Don't interrupt. Be patient and listen.

Validate: Acknowledge their feelings; it does not mean you agree.

Easy Manner: Empower, reassure, encourage, support, empathize, and offer soft suggestions that include safety.

After a person has experienced trauma, this is when they need you the most. Be supportive and love on them. If they distance themselves from you, don't take it personally and give them some space and time. This is a form of showing your love and support. When they are ready, they will talk to you, or they may not. Regardless, pray for them and ensure that they know that you are there for them when they are ready.

Definitions

HUSH Topics:

Hush topics are those that individuals, families, and organizations have a hard time discussing, such as sexual assault, domestic violence, child sexual abuse, sex trafficking, sexual harassment, incest, etc.

Survivor: A person who can cope and grow after suffering a traumatic event.

Victim: A person harmed, injured, or killed as a result of a crime. A person harmed or injured may still be suffering and wounded mentally and/or physically.

Victimology: The study of the victims of crime and the psychological effects caused by their traumatic experiences.

Source: Webster's Dictionary

Domestic Violence:

Domestic violence is an intentional pattern of physical, emotional, economic, sexual, and other tactics to instill fear and to coerce intimate partners to act against their own will or best interests. The behavior can be subtle, with abusers using a variety of ways to gain control, including insulting their partners, controlling their contact with family members and friends or limiting how their partners can spend money. Abuse can worsen and become more frequent with consistent physical injuries, such as hitting or slapping, sexual assaults, or threats to their partner's safety.

5 Types of Domestic Abuse
Emotional abuse:

[Emotional abuse](#) is almost like brainwashing in that it is done to wear away at a victim's self-confidence. It can be [verbal abuse](#), such as your partner repeatedly criticizing, intimidating, or belittling you. It can also be [nonverbal abuse or coercive control,](#) when your partner asserts control and tries to demean you by making decisions on your behalf. This can include anything from what you should wear to who your friends should be.

Financial abuse:

This type of abuse involves stealing or withholding money from the victim or using the victim's name and personal information to accrue debt. The victim may feel financially dependent on their partner, even to the point where they feel obligated to be submissive, or as though they are being forced to support their partner financially.

Physical abuse: This is the use of physical force against another person to inflict injury or put the person at risk of becoming injured. This may include your partner pushing, hitting, choking, or threatening you with a weapon.

Sexual abuse: This abuse often occurs in tandem with physical abuse. It involves forcing or coercing a victim to do something sexually, which can range from unwanted kissing or touching to rape. This can also involve threatening someone to perform a sexual act, including oral sex, restricting a victim's access to birth control and condoms, or repeatedly using sexual insults to demean a victim.

Spiritual abuse: It is also referred to as religious abuse. This involves a partner not allowing you to practice your moral or religious beliefs. It can include humiliation or harassment as a means of control, forcing a victim to give up their culture or values that are important to them. Spiritual abuse can be used by religious leaders to instill fear or guilt into a victim, coercing them to behave a certain way.

Source: Domesticshelters.org

Intimate Partner Violence (IPV):

Societal perspectives have expanded to understand better the types of violence that exist within relationships as well as the reality that the roles of abuser and victim are not gender-specific. As a result, the term "intimate partner violence" has been introduced to encompass a broader understanding of violence in relationships.

The concept of intimate partner violence acknowledges that abuse can exist in any intimate relationship, regardless of sexual orientation, marital status, or gender. Like "domestic violence," this new term does not confine the roles of abuser and victim to just one gender.

Source: https://inpublicsafety.com/2015/10/domestic-violence-and- intimate-partner-violence-whats-the-difference/

Sexual Assault: This term that refers to unwanted sexual acts against or without a person's consent. This includes any sexual, physical, verbal, or visual act that forces a person to engage in sexual contact against their will or without their consent. Sexual assault and rape may sometimes overlap and be used interchangeably in some circumstances. However, it is best to consult laws set at the state level to determine the exact difference between the two as this may vary depending on the jurisdiction.

Source: Raiin.org

Rape: The penetration, no matter how slight, of the vagina or anus with any body part or object, or oral penetration by a sex organ of another person, without the consent of the victim.

This definition includes any gender of victim and perpetrator, not just women being raped by men. It also recognizes that rape with an object can be as traumatic as penile/vaginal rape. This definition also includes instances in which the victim is unable to give consent because of temporary or permanent mental or physical incapacity. Furthermore, because many rapes are facilitated by drugs or alcohol, the new definition recognizes that a victim can be incapacitated and thus unable to consent because of ingestion of drugs or alcohol. Similarly, a victim may be legally incapable of consent because of age. The ability of the victim to give consent must be determined by the state statutes.

Physical resistance is not required on the part of the victim to demonstrate lack of consent.

Source: Department of Justice

Sexual Harassment: Repeated, uninvited contact (verbal, physical, or otherwise) against another person, like an applicant or an employee, of a sexual nature falls under the category of sexual harassment. This is defined as any unwelcome sexual advances, requests for sexual favors, and other verbal or physical harassment of a sexual form.

Visit https://www.eeoc.gov/employees/howtofile.cfm to file a complaint against an employer for discrimination, including discrimination as a result of your unwillingness to perform any sexual favors or stay quiet in the face of sexual harassment. Complaints can be filed online, in person, or via mail. Individuals have 180 days to file a claim.

Source: Equal Employment Opportunity Commission (EEOC)

Child Sexual Abuse: A form of child abuse that includes sexual activity with a minor. A child cannot consent to any form of sexual activity, period. When a perpetrator engages with a child this way, they are committing a crime that can have long-lasting effects on the victim. Child sexual abuse does not need to include physical contact between a perpetrator and a child. Some forms of child sexual abuse include:

- Exhibitionism, or exposing oneself to a minor

- Fondling
- Intercourse
- Masturbation in the presence of a minor or forcing the minor to masturbate
- Obscene phone calls, text messages, or digital interaction
- Producing, owning, or sharing pornographic images or movies of children
- Sex of any kind with a minor, including vaginal, oral, or anal
- Sex trafficking
- Any other sexual conduct that is harmful to a child's mental, emotional, or physical welfare

Child abuse perpetrator: A perpetrator does not have to be an adult to harm a child. They can have any relationship with the child including as an older sibling or playmate, family member, teacher, coach, neighbor, instructor, caretaker, or parent of another child.

The majority of perpetrators are someone the child or family knows. We highly recommend that parents be careful about who is allowed to spend time unsupervised with their children.

Source: Rainn.org

Incest: The sexual abuse of a person by a family member or a primary caregiver such as a stepparent. The abuse can occur as a child or adult. The abuse can be non-touching behavior such as exposure to another child, making a child watch pornography, invading privacy, taking explicit photos, or communicating with a child about sexual fantasies. The perpetrator can be an adult or older child.

Source: IncestAware.org

Sex trafficking: Sex trafficking is a form of modern-day slavery in which individuals perform commercial sex through the use of force, fraud, or coercion. Minors under the age of eighteen engaging in commercial sex are considered to be victims of human trafficking, regardless of the use of force, fraud, or coercion. Sex trafficking often takes the form of escort service, nonconsensual pornography, illicit massage businesses, brothels, and the outdoor solicitation of prostitution or any services of a sexual nature.

Source: polarisproject.org

Support Hotline Numbers

Feeling overwhelmed? There are a lot of phone numbers on this page. If you don't know where to start, call 2-1-1 or 9-8-8 on your phone to be connected with the National Human Service Center or HUSH No More at 1-888-285-2161. Contact 9-1-1 for all emergencies.

SEXUAL ASSAULT

National Sexual Assault Hotline 1-800-656-HOPE (4673)

DOD Safe Helpline 1-877-995-5247 (Military)

National Child Abuse Helpline 1-800-4-A-CHILD (422-4453)
Comfort In The Storm 562-547-5064

ADDICTION

Drug Abuse Helpline 1-800-662-4357
Alcoholic Anonymous 1-212-870-3400

DOMESTIC VIOLENCE

National Domestic Violence Hotline 1-800-799-SAFE (7233)
National Domestic Violence Hotline (Spanish) 1-800-942-6908
Battered Women and Their Children 1-800-603-HELP (4357)
Elder Abuse Hotline 1-800-252-8966

Family Violence Prevention Center 1-800-313-1310

SUICIDE

Suicide Hotline 1-800- 784-2433)/1-800-273-TALK (8255)

Suicide Prevention Hotline 1-800-827-7571

VA Suicide Helpline 1-855-302-6626

CHRISTIAN COUNSELING

National Prayer Line 1-800-4-PRAYER (772937)

Grace Help Line 24 HRs Christian Service 1- 800-982-8032

About the Author

Dr. Vanessa Dunn Guyton is the Founder and Executive Director of HUSH No More, a non-profit organization and movement that provides a platform to allow Survivors to share their story and help victims to heal and unleash the shame of their trauma. This platform led to her creating the HUSH No More Book, HUSH No More Trauma Releasing Coloring Book, and producing the HUSH No More Documentary. Her documentary has been shown internationally in Korea, Japan, Kuwait, Jordan, and Qatar to bring awareness to the HUSH Topics.

Additionally, she is the CEO of Consulting Experts & Associates, LLC. CEA is a global training consulting firm that assists organizations in improving training and organization effectiveness. Dr. Guyton honorably served in the United States Army as a Human Resource Specialist for ten years. Additionally, she is a credentialed Victim Advocate and has certified over 4,200 Sexual Assault Response Coordinators and Victim Advocates. Her training is provided globally to thousands of military organizations, colleges, and corporations on The Hush Topics.

Dr. Guyton is the proud mother of five children, Keith, Teaira, Tony, Miata, De'Quan and a Gigi to Braylin, Jeremiah, and Phoenix.

Follow and Connect with Dr. Guyton

linktr.ee/drguyton

www.hushnomore.org

https://www.facebook.com/hushnomoremovement/

https://www.instagram.com/hushnomorenow/

www.vanessaguyton.com

https://www.facebook.com/DrVanessaGuyton/

https://www.linkedin.com/in/dr-vanessa-dunn-guyton-ba818314 www.consultingexp.com

https://www.facebook.com/TheConsultingExpert/

https://twitter.com/ConsultingX

Contributing Authors:

Tammy Nicole Myers

Tammy Nobles

Jacqueline Renee Gonder

LeDesma "Desi" Terry

Eddie "Obbie West" Wilson

AmyAnna Soto

Sarah Vanalstyne

Scharnelle L. Hamlin

Tara Rivers

Kim Hardy

Best Boy

Debra Monk

Jessica Lewis

Serenity Carino

Maria Socolof

Annalee Somerville

Nikki Kelly

Amber

Angel Power

Teaira Mack

Robin D. Whitehead Rudolph

THANK YOU for supporting Dr. Guyton &

HUSH No More!!

Proceeds from the sale of this book support HUSH No More, a 501c3 nonprofit organization.

Donations are used to support Survivors and provide training around the world on

The HUSH Topics.

Made in United States
Orlando, FL
11 April 2024